JENNY BRISTOW

cooks for the seasons
spring and summer

JENNY BRISTOW

cooks for the seasons

spring and summer

THE
BLACKSTAFF
PRESS

BELFAST

IN ASSOCIATION WITH UTV

contents

I always look forward to the start of spring and to those bright March days when the sun feels warmer and that wintery chill has left the air. The days become longer and all around us plants and flowers are starting to bud. That feeling of energy and change comes into the kitchen too, as we leave behind the heavier foods of winter and look forward to all the wonderful spring produce. Tender pink stalks of rhubarb, the first of the asparagus and spring lamb are just a few of the treats you'll find. I've brought them together for you in a fabulous Easter lunch that includes a warm salad of asparagus with buttery lemon grass sauce and vanilla mousse with spring rhubarb. Of course, Easter wouldn't be the same without some chocolate indulgence, so I've included a recipe for a layered chocolate cake – the perfect finale to your meal!

As spring gives way to the long hot days of summer, life takes on a slower pace and we spend more time outdoors. Now is the perfect opportunity to get together with friends and family for barbecues and picnics. To help you make the most of these occasions, I've included a special section on alfresco eating that's packed full of practical advice and ideas for dips, marinades and dressings. My chick pea and herb burgers and my garlic and saffron prawn kebabs are guaranteed to add spice and sizzle to your barbecue. Of course, if you only turn up at pudding time, you won't be disappointed – my foil-wrapped fruit parcels are a real barbecue treat.

One of the reasons eating outdoors is so popular is that it has a holiday feel and it should come as no surprise that this book is dominated by the flavours, colours and aromas of the Mediterranean. So why not treat your friends and family to a special Mediterranean lunch. Start with mussels or a roasted couscous salad with summer vegetables or maybe a goats cheese, sundried tomato and basil tart. And how about a zesty lemon and vanilla tart to finish?

And when you've done with all the cooking, what better way to wind down than to fix yourself a mint julep or a tall glass of homemade lemonade, find yourself a sunny spot in the garden and relax. Take my advice, and make the most of these halcyon days, because it will be another year before they're back again!

Jenny Bristow

conversion tables

volume

1 tsp	5ml
1 dsp	10ml
1 tbsp	15ml
55ml	2floz
75ml	3floz
125ml	4floz
150ml	$1/4$pt
275ml	$1/2$pt
425ml	$3/4$pt
570ml	1pt
1 litre	$1^3/4$pt

oven temperatures

degrees centigrade	gas mark
140°	1
150°	2
170°	3
180°	4
190°	5
200°	6
220°	7
230°	8
240°	9

weights

grams	ounces
10g	$1/2$oz
25g	1oz
40g	$1^1/2$oz
50g	2oz
60g	$2^1/2$oz
75g	3oz
110g	4oz
125g	$4^1/2$oz
150g	5oz
175g	6oz
200g	7oz
225g	8oz
250g	9oz
275g	10oz
350g	12oz
400g	14oz
450g	1lb
700g	$1^1/2$lb
900g	2lb
1.3kg	3lb
1.8kg	4lb
2.3kg	5lb

measurements

millimetres	inches
3mm	$1/8$ inch
5mm	$1/4$ inch
1cm	$1/2$ inch
2cm	$3/4$ inch
2.5cm	1 inch
3cm	$1^1/4$ inches
4cm	$1^1/2$ inches
4.5cm	$1^3/4$ inches
5cm	2 inches
7.5cm	3 inches
10cm	4 inches
13cm	5 inches
15cm	6 inches
18cm	7 inches
20cm	8 inches
23cm	9 inches
25cm	10 inches
28cm	11 inches
30cm	12 inches

alfresco

One of the things I love most about spring and summer is the chance to get out of the kitchen to cook and eat outdoors. By some strange magic, food tastes that little bit better when eaten out of doors and a few rays of sunshine certainly improve the appetite! Whether you are having a barbecue, cooking a meal or going off on a picnic, the whole point about this style of eating is that it's relaxed and informal.

This section is designed to help you make the most of alfresco eating, with tips and hints on making the best of your barbecue and with great recipes for dips, marinades, kebabs and burgers, exactly the kind of food that works well outdoors.

Here are a few tips on how to get the best out of your barbecue.

1   Buy good quality equipment – gadgets with flimsy handles are dangerous.

2   Make sure the grill is scrubbed well with a wire brush. This helps prevent the food from sticking.

3   Do as much preparation as possible before cooking.

4   You do not need a lot of equipment, however, I recommend the following:

   • a stiff wire brush to clean the grill

   • spatulas and long-handled tongs – these are vital for turning food as often a fork will prick the food and let out the juices

   • hinged racks for fish and burgers

   • a firm bristled brush (not nylon) to coat and marinate food

   • metal skewers or wooden kebab sticks should be square or rectangular in shape as food often twists or slips on round skewers. If using wooden or bamboo skewers they must be soaked in cold water for at least 30 minutes before use to prevent them catching light.

barbecue

- oven gloves or padded mitts and an apron are good to have at hand

- a water spray is a handy safety device in case of flare-ups

5 Allow approximately 30 minutes between lighting the barbecue and beginning to cook. The secret to barbecueing well lies in having the coals at the right temperature. The best time to cook is when a good heat has developed and the coals are starting to glow and turn grey.

6 For extra flavour and aroma scatter an assortment of garden herbs on the barbecue coals. The 'woody' types, such as thyme and rosemary, work well.

7 Buy mesquite or hickory wood chips and place on top of the coals. This will give food a great flavour.

marinades and dressings

A few basic ingredients for good marinades are balsamic vinegar, lime juice and olive oil.

Marinades can only do what you let them, so the more time a marinade has to work, the better. Yet, in the case of an impromptu barbecue, time is often short so we resort to sauces, flavoured butters, dressings and dips to give barbecued food extra flavour.

Often we rely on fragrant fruit vinegars, expecially balsamic vinegar; oils such as walnut and hazelnut; zest of citrus fruits like lemon and lime; and lots of fresh and dried herbs and exotic spices. Good quality saffron and cardamom are two of my favourites for giving dressings a fabulous flavour and colour.

Marinades that double as sauces when reheated are invaluable, even though you may need to add a few extra ingredients to change the consistency. In fact, the flavour of a marinade is often enhanced when it is heated and cooked.

4

summer glaze for barbecued food

2 tbsp maple syrup or honey
2 tbsp mango chutney
1 tbsp chopped parsley
black pepper

Mix all the ingredients in a saucepan. Heat the glaze gently for 1 minute then use to brush over the top of any cooked food just before serving. This glaze can be used hot or cold.

lemon, garlic and ginger marinade

2 tbsp root ginger – finely chopped
3 cloves garlic – crushed
2 tbsp soy sauce
1 tbsp balsamic vinegar
1 lemon – zest and juice
1 tsp chilli sauce

Mix all the ingredients in a bowl and add the meat or fish of your choice. Leave it in the marinade for as long as possible – 30 minutes at least.

lime and cinnamon marinade

2 limes – zest and juice
125ml/4floz white wine
2 cinnamon sticks – halved
1 tbsp honey

Place all the ingredients in a large shallow dish and mix well. If possible, heat the ingredients in a saucepan for 1 minute – this intensifies the flavour – allow to cool, then pour the mixture over your meat or fish. Leave to marinate for at least 15–30 minutes before cooking.

vegetables

Whether it is sweet potatoes or corn, aubergines or courgettes, vegetables taste delicious when cooked on a grill over a bed of hot coals. The simple approach is best – try bulbs of garlic cut in half, sprinkled with olive oil and black pepper, or small onions roasted whole. Or sprinkle assorted peppers, chilli peppers, asparagus spears and large chunks of red onion with olive oil, garnish with a few herbs such as rosemary, basil or thyme and leave them to blacken and sweeten on the barbecue. Baby potatoes are delicious when sprinked with thyme and tarragon as are buttered courgettes with Italian parsley. If you are short of time, or if you have a lot of vegetables to cook, start them off in a roasting dish in the oven, then transfer them to foil and finish them off on the coals.

Vegetable kebabs are another great idea. They look stunning, require little preparation and can be served on their own or as an accompaniment to fish or meat. Choose your vegetables carefully so that they all cook at the same rate and will be tender at the same time. Be sure to cut them into even-sized chunks.

basil buttered corn on the cob

6 corn on the cob
50g/2oz butter
10–12 basil leaves – shredded
salt and black pepper

Discard the husks and boil or steam the corn for 6–7 minutes. In a separate bowl mix together the butter with the finely shredded basil leaves and black pepper. Drain the corn from the water, pat dry and spread each cob with basil butter. Place the corn cobs around the edge of the barbecue when the heat is low and cook for approximately 10 minutes until tender and slightly roasted. Serve hot with extra basil butter.

Use the dressings, dips and flavoured butters in this section to spice up your vegetables and to bring out their flavour.

Here's one idea. Thread cherry tomatoes, 1-inch cubes of onion, courgettes and red or yellow peppers onto wooden kebab sticks (these should be soaked in cold water for 30 minutes before use to prevent them catching alight). Crush about 15–20 leaves of basil and 1 clove of chopped garlic in a pestle and mortar. Add 4 dsp of olive oil and mix well. Brush the kebabs with the basil oil and cook on the barbecue until the vegetables are tender. Turn the kebabs frequently and keep brushing them with the oil during cooking. To serve, drizzle the vegetables with a little of the oil. Alternatively, you can replace with basil oil with green pesto which is readily available in jars in the supermarket.

chick pea and herb burgers

makes 8–10 burgers

Vegetarian burgers are delicious and can be made using all kinds of ingredients. For a change try replacing the chick peas with chopped mushrooms or lentils. Be careful not to make the burgers too big as they may break up.

1 tin chick peas
1 dsp olive oil
2 onions – finely chopped
2 cloves garlic – finely chopped
50g/2oz chopped almonds
2 dsp fresh herbs, e.g. basil, parsley, oregano – finely chopped
salt and freshly ground black pepper
2 eggs – lightly beaten
50g/2oz plain flour
110g/4oz breadcrumbs

1   Drain and mash the chick peas to a soft purée. In a shallow pan heat the oil and add the onion and garlic. Cook for 2–3 minutes until softened. Add the chick pea purée and continue cooking for a further 2 minutes. Add the chopped almonds and herbs and mix well. Season with salt and freshly ground black pepper.

2   Transfer the mixture to a bowl and allow to cool slightly. Add 1 egg and mix well to bind the ingredients. Now use a tablespoon or your hands to shape the mixture into round patties.

3   Coat the burgers lightly in flour and dip into the remaining lightly beaten egg. Finally toss the burgers in breadcrumbs. Pat down well, then leave to cool before cooking on the barbecue for approximately 10 minutes.

7

kebabs

sizzling garlic and saffron prawns

makes 6–8 kebabs

900g/2lb large shelled prawns
10–12 saffron threads
2 dsp olive oil
4 cloves garlic – finely chopped
2 dsp spring onions – finely chopped
1 red chilli – deseeded and finely chopped
1 lemon and 1 lime – sliced

1   Bring a large pan of salted water to the boil and add the prawns. Cook for 4–5 minutes, drain and put to one side.

2   Grind the saffron to a powder in a pestle and mortar. Add 2 dsp of hot water and leave to infuse for 3–4 minutes.

3   Mix the olive oil, garlic, spring onions and chilli in a bowl. Add the saffron mixture and the prawns. Mix well and leave for 30 minutes to let the flavours infuse and develop.

4   Thread the prawns onto skewers, along with some slices of lemon and lime. Cook on the barbecue for 4–5 minutes just to heat through.

Serve immediately with salad or crusty bread.

spicy beef kebabs

makes 6–8 kebabs

1/2 tsp turmeric
1/2 tsp cinnamon
1 dsp basil – finely chopped
1 dsp parsley – finely chopped
2 dsp soy sauce
1 dsp balsamic vinegar
1 tsp sesame oil
700g/1 1/2lb steak pieces
225g/8oz large salad onions
basil leaves – coarsely shredded

1   Mix the turmeric, cinnamon, basil, parsley, soy sauce, balsamic vinegar and sesame oil in a large bowl. Add the steak pieces, cover the bowl with cling film and leave to marinate for 30–45 minutes.

2   Remove the steak pieces and set the marinade to one side. Thread alternate pieces of steak and whole salad onions onto skewers.

3   Place the kebabs on a grill over the hot coals and cook until the meat is golden and tender. Brush the kebabs occasionally with the marinade during cooking.

When cooked, sprinkle the kebabs with basil and serve at once.

sweet chilli sauce

This is an irresistible sauce for any cooked meat and one that is guaranteed to add some zing. Increase the quantity of chillies if you like your sauce really hot.

4–6 red or green chillies – deseeded and finely chopped
225g/8oz granulated sugar
275ml/^{1}/2pt white wine vinegar
110g/4oz sultanas – finely chopped
4 cloves garlic – crushed
pinch of salt
1 tbsp root ginger – grated

Place all the ingredients in a large saucepan. Bring to the boil and simmer gently with the lid off for 30 minutes. This will give the sultanas time to soften and will reduce the strength of the vinegar.

The sauce can be served as it is or it can be blended if you prefer a smoother texture. Serve hot or cold.

parsley, mustard and green peppercorn butter

Almost anything can be used to flavour butter – mustard, black pepper, herbs, spices, chillies and even cheeses. Vary the quantity to suit your own taste.

Flavoured butters are an excellent way to add moisture and flavour to grilled food which can easily toughen during cooking. The butter can be made well in advance and then sliced and placed on top of cooked food to provide an attractive sauce.

Mix 110g/4oz of softened unsalted butter with 1 tsp of grainy mustard, 1 dsp coarsely chopped parsley and some freshly ground green peppercorns. When all the ingredients have been thoroughly mixed into the butter and the mixture is relatively smooth, transfer it to a piece of foil. Roll the butter into the shape of a log and chill in the fridge until it is time for it to be used. To serve, cut into slices and place on top of grilled food.

9

dips

guacamole

This simple dip is fresh, tasty and easy to make and is always popular with guests. Mexican in origin, guacamole works best with spicy tortillas, but it is also good with bread or crackers. It can also serve as a sauce to accompany chicken. Make guacamole as close as possible to the time it will be served – it may discolour if the avocados are very ripe.

2 avocados – stoned, peeled and roughly chopped
¹/2 onion – finely chopped
2 green chillies – deseeded and finely chopped
1 tbsp coriander – finely chopped
1 tbsp lime juice
salt and freshly ground black pepper

1   When you have removed the large stones from the avocados, wash the stones and set them to one side.

2   Mash the flesh of the avocado and add the onion, chillies, coriander and lime juice. Mix well and season.

3   Place the avocado stones in the guacamole and cover with clingfilm. This will help prevent any browning. Remove the stone before serving.

Serve as soon as possible.

jerked honey dip

1 tsp jerked seasoning
125ml/4floz honey
4 tbsp soy sauce
1 tsp dark rum
1 tsp chilli sauce
25g/1oz soft brown sugar

1   Place all the ingredients in a saucepan and mix well. Bring to the boil and cook for 2 minutes.

2   Remove from the heat and serve either hot or cold with cooked meats, especially chicken or roasted vegetables. This dip also works well with crudites and can even be used as a marinade.

Don't forget toasted marshmallows on kebab sticks for the kids!

As the embers die on the barbecue and while there is still a reasonable heat in the coals, you can create simple no fuss desserts that will round off your alfresco meal perfectly.

Foil-wrapped sliced fruits tossed in liqueur and a little brown sugar can be delicious. Try chopped bananas, peaches and nectarines, tossed in brown sugar with a little peach schnapps and cooked in the same way as the baked berries below.

- Griddle cakes and pancakes are delicious on the barbecue. Heat for 1–2 minutes on both sides and served with butter or syrup.
- Fruits can be cooked on kebab sticks. Plums, nectarines, peaches and pineapple work well. Cut into chunks, sprinkle with brown sugar or drizzle with honey and cook for 2–3 minutes until caramelised.
- Baked whole apples with blackcurrants are a favourite of mine. Simply core an apple and fill it with blackcurrants and a little brown sugar. Wrap in foil and cook on the barbecue for 12–15 minutes, or until soft.

baked berries

Place an assortment of berried fruits into individual foil parcels e.g. strawberries, raspberries, cherries, redcurrants and blueberries. Sprinkle with 25g/1oz of brown sugar and a little fresh orange juice or liqueur e.g. kirsch or brandy. Take care to completely seal the parcels so that they will not leak. Cook on the barbecue for approximately 5 minutes until the fruit is bubbling and the sugar dissolved. Serve with whipped cream, yoghurt or a small spoonful of mascarpone.

11

snacks
soups
salads

whole roasted garlic soda bread

makes one loaf

This is one of the nicest ways to cook garlic – roasting the cloves whole in the oven gives them a sweeter flavour and a softer texture.

1 bulb garlic
pinch of salt
2 dsp olive oil

1 Cut the top off the bulb of garlic and place it on a baking sheet. Sprinkle with the salt and olive oil. Roast in the oven @ 200°C/gas mark 6 for 35–40 minutes or until the garlic is soft and the pulp is easily squeezed out (roasting time will depend on the size of the bulb). Keep an eye on the garlic towards the end of cooking, as burnt garlic is bitter and inedible.

2 Remove the garlic from the oven. Peel off the papery layers and use a fork to mash the now softened garlic.

450g/1lb plain flour
1tsp salt
1 tsp baking soda
1–2 dsp olive oil
425ml/³/4pt buttermilk
1 egg – lightly beaten

3 Sieve the flour, salt and baking soda into a bowl. Add the roasted garlic purée and olive oil. Pour most of the buttermilk in at once and mix to a soft dough using either your hands or a spatula. Add more buttermilk as necessary.

4 Turn the dough onto a floured board and knead gently so that it comes together without any cracks. Shape into a round (approximately 3–4cm/1¹/4–1¹/2 inches deep) and score a cross on top. Brush with the egg and cook in the oven @ 200°C/gas mark 6 for at least 20 minutes or until fully cooked. When ready, the bread should be golden brown in colour and sound hollow when tapped on the bottom. Best eaten warm, fresh from the oven.

As a variation, try Mediterranean soda bread – simply add 4–5 chopped sundried tomatoes and 25g/1oz toasted pine nuts, or 1 dsp olive oil and 25g/1oz pitted black olives, instead of roasted garlic. Another alternative is garden herb soda bread – replace the garlic with 1 dsp finely chopped basil, chives or coriander.

mid-season minestrone

serves 6–8

There are many ways to make minestrone. My version has all the essential ingredients – beans, garlic and tomatoes – but is more luxurious and packed full of freshness. The secret of this soup is not to overcook the pasta and vegetables.

110g/4oz white haricot beans
1 dsp olive oil
1 large onion – finely chopped
2 carrots – diced
3 celery sticks – sliced
3 cloves garlic – chopped

2 litres/3¹/2pt chicken or vegetable stock
6–8 basil leaves – finely shredded
4 large tomatoes – skinned, deseeded and diced
salt and freshly ground black pepper
2 courgettes – finely diced
110g/4oz freshly podded peas
4 asparagus tips
50g/2oz French beans – chopped
50g/2oz pasta – vermicelli or broken spaghetti
2 tsp green pesto
110g/4oz Parmesan/pecorino cheese

1 If using dried beans soak in cold water overnight, drain and rinse well. Place in a saucepan with sufficient cold water to cover them, bring to the boil and cook for 2 hours until they soften. Drain and leave to cool. Alternatively, use the tinned variety which do not require any cooking.

2 Heat the oil in a large heavy-based pan and add the onion, carrots, celery and garlic. Cover and cook gently for 10–12 minutes until vegetables have softened.

3 Add the stock to the pot along with the basil, tomatoes, haricot beans and seasoning. Cook for 20–25 minutes. Add the courgettes, peas, asparagus, French beans and pasta, and simmer gently for 10–12 minutes until the vegetables have softened.

4 Before serving add the pesto and mix well. Sprinkle with Parmesan and serve at once with warm crusty bread.

tip

The easiest way to skin a tomato is to make a few incisions into the skin with a knife, then place it in a cup of boiling water for approximately 30 seconds until the skin begans to peel off.

summer soup of favas, basil and brie

serves 6–8

This is a delicious soup with good colour and a fresh taste. It can be made with both the fava beans and their pods, if they are young and tender. Feel free to vary the dish by changing the choice of herb, but I think this combination of favas – also known as broad beans – basil and Brie is hard to beat.

900g/2lb fava beans in the pod

1 If the beans are young and tender, chop them in their pods. If they are well ripened, shell them.

1–2 dsp olive oil
1 onion – finely chopped
2 cloves garlic – roasted
2–3 potatoes – peeled and diced

2 Heat the oil in a heavy-based pan and add the onion, garlic and potatoes. Sauté gently for 8–10 minutes, but do not allow to discolour. Add the sliced beans and continue cooking for 3–4 minutes.

2 litres/3¹/2pt chicken stock
salt and freshly ground black pepper

3 Pour the stock over the beans and season. Cover and simmer gently for 12–15 minutes, until all the vegetables are soft but still a good bright colour. Remove from the heat, allow to cool slightly, and then blitz in the blender.

8–10 leaves fresh basil – finely shredded
110g/4oz Brie – sliced

4 Return the soup to the pan and add the basil. Heat through and serve with slices of Brie on top. A few fresh shredded leaves of basil can be used to garnish the soup.

ribbon egg and crouton salad
with a green pesto dressing

serves 6

This is an excellent salad for a picnic. It can be made up in advance and the dressing stored in an airtight jar and poured just before serving.

1 pkt lambs lettuce
$^1/_2$ cucumber – diced
110g/4oz garlic croutons
50g/2oz Mediterranean olives
1 dsp spring onions – sliced

Arrange the salad ingredients in a bowl.

green pesto dressing

4 tbsp olive oil
1 tbsp white wine vinegar
1 tbsp green pesto
salt and freshly ground black pepper

Place the olive oil, white wine vinegar, pesto and seasoning in a bowl or in a screw top jar. Stir or shake well.

ribbon egg

3 eggs – lightly beaten
1 dsp cold water
1 tsp parsley – finely chopped
25g/1oz butter
1 dsp olive oil

1 Mix the eggs with the water and parsley.

2 Heat the butter and oil in a large frying pan. Add the egg mixture and cook over a high temperature for 2–3 minutes until set. There is no need to turn it. Ease out onto a board or plate and leave to cool.

3 Cut the eggs into ribbon slices and arrange over the salad. Drizzle with the pesto dressing and serve at once.

summer salad of iceberg lettuce
with a sweet poppy seed dressing

serves 6–8

Crisp and fresh, iceberg lettuce is perfect for a summer salad. This sweet poppy seed dressing is one of the nicest dressings I've tasted and the crunchy texture of the seeds works a treat with the lettuce.

1 iceberg lettuce

1   Prepare the lettuce by washing the leaves well, drying and arranging in a serving bowl.

4 dsp olive or grapeseed oil
4 dsp white wine vinegar
1 small white onion – finely chopped
2 dsp caster sugar
$^1/_2$ tsp dried mustard
salt and freshly ground black pepper
1 tsp poppy seeds

2   Place the oil, white wine vinegar, onion, caster sugar, mustard and seasoning into a blender. Pulse until the dressing is well mixed. Add the poppy seeds and mix by hand.

3   Pour the dressing over the lettuce and serve at once.

greek yoghurt and
aromatic ginger dressing

Another dressing that works well. Its creamy texture and sharp flavour are a perfect foil to the crispness of the lettuce.

150ml/$^1/_4$ pt Greek set yoghurt
1 tbsp honey
zest and juice of $^1/_2$ lemon
1 inch root ginger – finely chopped or crushed
$^1/_2$ tsp English mustard
1 tsp spring onions – very finely chopped

Mix all the ingredients together, adding the spring onions at the very end. Serve chilled.

23

prawn and salmon open sandwich in a filo crust

serves 6–8

This delicate sandwich is easy to make but looks impressive and tastes delicious. It's ideal if you are having friends or family for lunch.

6–8 sheets filo pastry
25g/1oz melted butter

Defrost the filo pastry and brush each layer with the melted butter, layering a greased rectangular (30 x 10cm/12 x 4 inches) or round (20cm/8 inch) tin as you go along. Press carefully into the edges.

filling

150ml/¹/4pt yoghurt
3 egg yolks
4 dsp cream – single or double
110–175g/4–6oz fresh salmon – finely sliced
75g/3oz shelled prawns
¹/4 cucumber – peeled and diced
1 dsp parsley or dill
1 tsp peppercorns – crushed

1   Mix together the yoghurt and egg yolks. Beat for 1 minute, then add the cream.

2   Place the salmon, prawns, cucumber and herbs on the base of the flan. Pour the sauce over the filling. Sprinkle with the peppercorns and bake in the oven @ 200°C/gas mark 6 for 15–18 minutes or until firm to the touch.

Cut into slices and serve.

chicken, coconut and galangal soup

serves 6–8

This Thai-style soup uses galangal, a hot peppery spice belonging to the ginger family. You can buy it either fresh or dried in Asian foodstores. Use the fresh variety if you can.

570ml/1pt chicken stock
1 stalk lemon grass – finely chopped
1 inch galangal – cut and finely sliced
2 kaffir lime leaves
4 tbsp lime juice
4 tbsp fish sauce

1 Pour the chicken stock into a large saucepan. It is important to use fresh stock. This is relatively easy to make (see below) and can also be bought from some supermarkets. Add the lemon grass, galangal, lime leaves, lime juice and fish sauce. Bring to the boil and simmer gently for 5–6 minutes to release the flavours.

900g/2lb chicken fillets –
cut into strips
150ml/1/4pt coconut milk
2 red and 2 green chillies –
deseeded and finely chopped
a few fresh coriander leaves – torn

2 Add the chicken strips and the coconut milk to the stock. Simmer for 10–12 minutes until the chicken is cooked. Add the chillies and coriander leaves. Heat through and serve.

galangal strips – cut into fine strips
3 red and 3 green chillies –
finely shredded

3 Deep-fry the galangal strips and chillies for 2–3 minutes until they become crispy. Serve as a garnish to the soup.

chicken stock

To make approximately 1.1 litres/2pt of stock, place 2 litres/3 1/2 pt of water; 1lb/450g of chicken joints; 1 leek – roughly chopped; 1 carrot and 1 onion – roughly chopped; 1 bay leaf and/or bunch of parsley; salt and freshly ground black pepper in a large saucepan and simmer gently over a low heat for 1–1 1/2 hours until the liquid has absorbed all the flavours. Skim off any fat with a ladle – it is easier to do this when the soup is cool – strain and use. The stock can be frozen for up to 6 months.

crunchy salad of rice noodles, radishes and summer vegetables
in a thai dressing

serves 8

This crunchy salad is a fresh and healthy option for summer. It is delicious on its own as a lunch dish, but works equally well as a side dish with chicken or fish.

225g/8oz rice noodles

1 Cook the noodles in boiling salted water for 4–5 minutes, or according to the instructions on the packet, then drain.

6–8 radishes – finely sliced
1 red and 1 green chilli – finely chopped
1 red and 1 green pepper – finely sliced
225g/8oz mangetout peas – lightly steamed for 2 mins
50g/2oz cashew nuts

2 Add the prepared vegetables to the noodles and mix carefully. Scatter the cashew nuts over the top of the salad.

dressing

6 tbsp lime juice
2 tbsp olive oil
1 tbsp light soy sauce
1 tsp sesame oil
1 tsp caster sugar
1 inch root ginger – finely chopped
1 chilli – finely chopped
1 clove garlic – crushed

Place all the ingredients for the dressing in a screw top jar and shake well. Drizzle over the salad immediately, while the noodles are still hot.

basil and coriander – finely shredded

Serve garnished with basil and coriander.

29

roasted couscous salad
with summer vegetables

serves 6–8

This is an ideal dish for vegetarians. It tastes delicious, looks stunning and can be made with whichever vegetables are in season.

275g/10oz couscous
570ml/1pt vegetable or chicken stock
salt and freshly ground black pepper

1 Place the couscous in a large bowl, pour in the stock and seasoning. Leave to infuse for 10 minutes until all the liquid is absorbed. Taste the couscous and if it is still slightly hard, add a little more hot stock and leave it to absorb.

1 aubergine – diced
1 courgette – diced
1 yellow and 1 red pepper – diced
225g/8oz baby tomatoes
1 red onion – sliced
2 cloves garlic – chopped
2 lemons – halved
6–8 basil leaves – shredded
2 dsp olive oil
salt and freshly ground black pepper

2 Place all the vegetables and the lemons on a roasting tin. Sprinkle with the basil, olive oil and seasoning. Place in the oven @ 200°C/gas mark 6 for 25–30 minutes or under a preheated grill for 12–15 minutes, turning often until the vegetables are golden and slightly crispy.

3 When the vegetables are cooked remove from the oven and squeeze the roasted lemon juice over the couscous and mix through. Toss the roasted vegetables through the couscous, transfer to a roasting dish and reheat in the oven for 6–7 minutes.

110g/4oz black olives
basil or coriander – chopped
4 dsp sundried tomato paste
2 dsp olive oil

4 Remove from the oven, add the olives and serve garnished with basil or coriander or a quick dressing made by mixing some sundried tomato paste and olive oil.

31

mussels in saffron broth

serves 6–8

When you are buying mussels, ensure they are tightly closed and have a fresh smell of the sea. The intense bitter flavour of the saffron works incredibly well with the mussels in this dish. It can be bought in powder form or as fine threads.

1kg/2.2lb fresh mussels

1 Scrub the mussels well and remove the beards. Tap any mussels that are open and discard if they do not close tightly. The clean, closed mussels should be left to steep in a basin of cold water for up to 1 hour.

4 spring onions – chopped
150–275ml/^{1}/4–^{1}/2pt dry white wine
0.9–1.4 litres/1^1/2–2^1/2pt fish stock
2–3 dsp parsley

2 Place the mussels in a large saucepan with the spring onions, wine, fish stock and parsley (there must be sufficient stock to cover the mussels). Cover with a lid and cook for 5–7 minutes until the mussels have opened. Drain off the liquid into a bowl or a jug and put to one side. Leave the mussels in the saucepan to cool slightly.

saffron broth

150ml/^{1}/4pt dry white wine
2–3 spring onions – finely chopped
8–10 saffron threads – placed in a few drops of hot water for 8–10 minutes
110g/4oz butter
3 dsp parsley
150ml/^{1}/4pt cooking liquid from cooked mussels

1 In a separate pan heat the wine, spring onions and saffron threads and cooking liquid from the mussels. Cook for 2–3 minutes until the liquid has reduced. Add the butter and parsley and heat through, stirring regularly.

2 The mussels can either be kept in their shells or removed from them. Pour the broth over the mussels and serve.

tip

A little cream can be added to the sauce to make it richer (approximately 150ml/^{1}/4pt).

aubergine relish
with bruschetta

serves 6

This spicy relish is ideal with toasted bruschetta and goes very well with the baked whole fish on page 59.

3–4 dsp olive oil
4 cloves garlic – chopped
1 onion – finely chopped

1 Heat the oil in a large frying pan. Add the garlic and onion and cook gently for 2–3 minutes.

1/2 tsp curry powder
1 tsp cumin powder
salt and freshly ground black pepper

2 Add the curry powder, cumin and seasoning and cook for a further 2 minutes.

3–4 aubergines – diced

3 Add the aubergines and cook for 5 minutes, stirring often.

juice of 1–2 lemons
1 tsp chilli sauce
50g/2oz soft brown sugar

4 Add the lemon juice, chilli sauce and brown sugar, cover and simmer over a gentle heat for 15 minutes. It is important to keep an eye on the relish as it should not be allowed to overcook and break up.

5 When cooked, remove from the heat, cool and store in the fridge until ready to use. It will keep for 1 week.

bruschetta

Every country has its own very special way of serving toasted bread, but the Italian bruschetta has it all – a good country style bread, flavoured with extra virgin olive oil and a hint of garlic. Unbeatable.

1–2 baguettes
3–4 dsp extra virgin olive oil
2–3 whole cloves garlic

1 Cut the bread in half lengthways and rub with the garlic. Sprinkle generously with olive oil.

2 Place the sliced bread, oiled side down, on a hot griddle pan or on the barbecue for approximately 2–3 minutes until golden brown.

Top with the aubergine relish.

35

savoury sandwich ideas

Choose an assortment of breads, split them down the centre and sprinkle with olive oil. Then simply choose one of the tasty options below.

1   Mix together 225g/8oz cooked shelled prawns with 1 dsp spring onions and 1 dsp lemon juice. Spread this over one half of the bread and top with a few fine slices of Brie. Close the sandwich over, wrap in tinfoil and place on the barbecue for 8–10 minutes to allow the prawns to heat and the cheese to melt. Alternatively, heat in an oven @ 200°C/gas mark 6 for 10–12 minutes.

2   Finely chop 225g/8oz lightly smoked undyed fish, for example, haddock or cod. Place on top of the bread and sprinkle with the cheese of your choice. Cook in a preheated oven @ 200°C/gas mark 6 for 15–20 minutes.

3   Mix 200g/7oz of finely chopped bacon rashers with 110g/4oz blue-veined cheese. Sprinkle on top of crusty bread and cook in a preheated oven @ 200°C/gas mark 6 for 15–20 minutes.

mediterranean crisps

Take 1–2 packets of any variety of crisps. Place the crisps on a sheet of tinfoil and sprinkle with either:

1   3–4 coarsely chopped gherkins and 110g/4oz melting cheese.

2   6–8 coarsely chopped sundried tomatoes and 110g/4oz sliced mozzarella. A few black or green olives can also be added.

Heat in the oven @ 200°C/gas mark 6 for a few minutes, or wrap in tinfoil and place on the barbecue.

main courses

herb flavoured fish pie with a flavoursome crust

serves 4

In this simple recipe the fish is poached gently, flavoured with cream, lemon and parsley, and topped with tasty sundried tomatoes, chopped anchovies and garlic croutons.

2 x 225g/8oz pieces of white fish,
e.g. haddock, cod, whiting
225g/8oz lightly smoked,
undyed haddock

1 Cut the fish evenly into large cubes. Ensure the fish is free of any bones.

275ml/¹/2pt milk
25g/1oz butter
salt and freshly ground black pepper
2 dsp cream
4 dsp crème fraîche
1 dsp parsley – finely chopped
110g/4oz garden peas – lightly cooked
zest of 1 lemon

2 Gently heat the milk and butter in a large shallow pan and add the seasoning and fish. Poach gently until the fish softens (this will take about 5 minutes). Add the cream and crème fraîche and lightly mix in with the fish until the sauce thickens. Scatter the parsley, peas and lemon zest over the fish but do not stir. Heat gently for 1–2 minutes – do not boil – then transfer to a serving dish.

topping

4 dsp olive oil
2 cloves garlic – finely chopped
3–4 anchovy fillets – finely chopped
3–4 sundried tomatoes – chopped
1 red and 1 green chilli –
finely chopped
350g/12oz bread – diced
juice of 1 large lemon
¹/2 tsp paprika pepper
50g/2oz Cheddar – coarsely grated

Heat the olive oil in a pan and add the garlic, anchovies, sundried tomatoes and chillies. Cook gently for no longer than 1–2 minutes. Add the bread and mix. Cook until the bread is coated and crispy. Add the lemon juice, paprika and cheese. Once the cheese starts to melt pour the mixture over the fish. Serve at once or brown under a hot grill.

tart of trout
with a parmesan crust

serves 6–8

This tart is great served hot or cold. The flavours are simple and tasty and the Parmesan gives an added 'bite'.

pastry

250g/9oz plain flour
125g/4^{1}/2oz butter
25g/1oz Parmesan – grated
salt and freshly ground black pepper
1 egg yolk
1 dsp cold water

1   Place the flour, butter, cheese and seasoning into a blender along with the egg yolk and water. Whiz until the mixture comes together. This should take just under a minute. Turn the dough out onto a floured board or counter, knead and roll out to line a lightly greased rectangular ovenproof dish, approximately 23 x 13cm/9 x 5 inches.

2   Line the dish carefully with the pastry, trying not to stretch it as this will cause it to shrink during cooking. Trim any excess pastry. Cover the dish with cling film and place in the fridge for 15 minutes.

filling

450g/1lb trout fillets
75–110g/3–4oz watercress
200g/7oz baby tomatoes
225ml/8floz double or soured cream
4 dsp yoghurt
5 eggs – lightly beaten
zest of 1 lemon
1 dsp chives – finely chopped
spring onions – roughly chopped

parsley – roughly chopped
slices of lemon

1   Skin the trout fillets and cut into small pieces.

2   Remove the pastry case from the fridge and arrange the trout in the bottom. Top with watercress and tomatoes.

3   In a bowl, mix together the cream, yoghurt, eggs, lemon zest, chives and spring onions. Pour this over the watercress and tomatoes and bake in the oven @ 180°C/gas mark 4–5 for 20–25 minutes until golden and firm to the touch.

Serve hot or cold garnished with parsley and lemon.

mediterranean chicken casserole

serves 8

This recipe brings together a combination of Mediterranean flavours and textures. The addition of coriander and flat leaf parsley just before serving gives the dish a wonderful freshness.

900g/2lb chicken fillets
4 cloves garlic – roasted
2 red and 2 green chillies – deseeded and finely chopped
1 dsp olive oil

1 Cut the chicken into long ribbon strips and place in a bowl with the garlic, chillies and olive oil. Mix well and cover with cling film. Leave to marinate for up to 1 hour.

1 dsp olive oil
4 red onions – sliced
900g/2lb ripe plum tomatoes – coarsely chopped
2 dsp red pesto
570ml/1pt chicken stock

2 Remove the chicken from the marinade. Place the olive oil in a large heavy-based pan and, when hot, add the chicken, in batches if necessary. Cook until golden and crispy. Next, add the red onion slices and continue cooking for 3–4 minutes until the onions become crispy. Add the plum tomatoes, pesto and stock and simmer gently over a low heat for 45 minutes, keeping the lid on.

200g/7oz tinned chick peas
110g/4oz pine nuts
110g/4oz black olives
2 dsp sundried tomato paste

3 Finally, add the chick peas, pine nuts, olives and sundried tomato paste and heat through for a further 8–10 minutes.

handful of coriander
handful of flat leaf parsley

Garnish with coriander and flat leaf parsley before serving.

45

goats cheese, sundried tomato and basil tart

serves 8

This is a simple vegetarian tart which can be varied with the addition of olives or leeks. Ham or bacon may also be added if you prefer.

500g/1.1lb ready-made shortcrust pastry

Defrost and roll out the pastry to line a greased flan dish (23–25cm/9–10 inches). Trim excess pastry, prick lightly with a fork and place in the fridge for 15 minutes. Remove from the fridge and bake blind (i.e. line the tart with greaseproof paper and scatter baking beans or dried beans over the base to hold the paper down, removing the paper and beans after 10 minutes) for 15 minutes @ 200°C/gas mark 6.

filling

4 eggs – lightly beaten
2 dsp single or (preferably) double cream
200ml/7floz crème fraîche
salt and freshly ground black pepper

1   Mix the eggs, cream and crème fraîche in a bowl. Season.

110g/4oz sundried tomatoes – chopped
110g/4oz baby tomatoes
10–12 basil leaves
225g/8oz goats cheese – chunks
50g/2oz fontina cheese – grated

2   Scatter the sundried tomatoes, baby tomatoes, basil and cheese evenly over the base of the tart. Pour the creamy sauce on top and bake in the oven @ 190°C/gas mark 5 for 20–25 minutes until cooked, golden and firm to the touch.

Serve with the roasted couscous salad and summer vegetables on page 31.

lemon cream tagliatelle
with courgettes, broad beans and herbs

serves 4–6

A quick and simple dish using the best of the season's greens. Bring this dish to life with a generous sprinkling of summer herbs.

450g/1lb tagliatelle

1 Cook the pasta in boiling salted water for 6–7 minutes. Do not overcook as it is important to serve the dish *al dente* (with a slight bite). Drain the pasta, cover, and set to one side. A little olive oil can be added to keep the pasta moist.

25g/1oz butter
1 dsp olive oil
2 cloves garlic – finely chopped
zest of 2 lemons
2 courgettes – finely sliced
110g/4oz broad beans
150ml/¼pt whipping cream
salt and freshly ground black pepper
1 dsp herbs – finely chopped e.g. coriander or parsley

2 Melt the butter and olive oil in a shallow pan. Add the garlic, lemon zest, courgettes and broad beans. Heat through and cook for 2–3 minutes.

3 Add the cream, seasoning, herbs and pasta and heat for a further 1–2 minutes.

75g/3oz Parmesan or pecorino cheese – optional

As a finishing touch, sprinkle with Parmesan or pecorino just before serving.

irish salmon
with a creamy chive sauce

serves 4

The best way of cooking salmon is to cook it simply with a little butter and lemon juice. A short cooking time also ensures that the best of the flavour is retained. This dish is served with an indulgently creamy chive sauce.

4 x 110g/4oz fillets of salmon
2 dsp lemon juice
salt and freshly ground black pepper

1 Trim the salmon fillets into neat, even sizes. Just before cooking, sprinkle with the lemon juice and season well.

275ml/^{1}/2pt water
125ml/4floz dry white wine
25g/1oz butter

2 Pour the water and wine into a baking tin. Place the salmon fillets skin side down in the tin, placing a knob of butter on top of each one. Cover the top of the baking tin tightly with tinfoil and cook for 10–12 minutes @ 190°C/gas mark 5. Remove the salmon from the tin and serve immediately with the chive sauce.

creamy chive sauce

25g/1oz butter
2–4 dsp dry white wine
150ml/^{1}/4pt whipping cream
1 small bunch chives – finely chopped

Heat the butter in a shallow pan and add the wine and cream and chives. Heat through and simmer for 2–3 minutes, stirring frequently. Serve alongside the salmon.

There are many accompaniments that would work well with this meal. See page 53 for some ideas.

tip
Add 2–3 dsp fish stock to the sauce when you add the wine and cream. This will give the dish extra flavour.

cucumber and vine tomato salsa

1 cucumber – peeled and diced
3 vine tomatoes – skinned, deseeded
and diced
110g/4oz black olives –
coarsely chopped
salt and freshly ground black pepper

Mix the vegetables in a bowl and leave for 30 minutes to let the flavours infuse. Season and serve.

wilted scallions, pak choi and leeks

10–12 scallions
6–8 heads pak choi
8–10 baby leeks
1 dsp olive oil
2 tbsp dark soy sauce
1 dsp honey
salt and freshly ground black pepper

1 Lightly steam all the vegetables for 2 minutes.

2 Heat the olive oil in a shallow frying pan, add the vegetables, soy sauce, honey and seasoning. Heat through for 1–2 minutes and serve.

griddled potatoes with lemon and yoghurt

4–6 small/medium potatoes
olive oil

150ml/¼pt low fat yoghurt
zest of 1 lemon
juice of ½ lemon
freshly ground black pepper
1dsp chopped herbs e.g. mint –
optional

1 Steam the potatoes for 5–6 minutes or boil gently for 4–5 minutes. Remove, pat dry and cut into slices approximately 1–1½cm thick.

2 Heat a griddle pan and brush lightly with olive oil. Arrange the potatoes and allow to blacken slightly for 2–3 minutes on each side.

3 Remove the potatoes and place in a bowl with the yoghurt, lemon zest and juice, seasoning and herbs. Toss gently and serve either hot or cold.

chiang mai pork curry and sticky rice

serves 8

A wonderfully hot and tasty curry with a fiery flavour. The sticky rice – a glutinous variety of rice frequently used in Thailand – is an ideal accompaniment and is available in most supermarkets.

2 pork fillets

1   Trim any visible fat from the fillets and cut them into fine slivers.

1 tbsp olive oil
2–3 cloves garlic –
coarsely chopped
2 tbsp red curry paste
275ml/^{1}/2pt coconut milk

2   Heat a wok until you can just about see smoke rising. Add the oil, garlic and curry paste and cook for a further 3–4 minutes to develop the flavour. Add the coconut milk, stir well and continue to simmer for 5 minutes.

125ml/4floz vegetable stock
1 inch root ginger –
finely chopped
2 tbsp fish sauce
1dsp soft brown sugar
1 tbsp turmeric
1 dsp lime juice

3   Add the pork slivers and stock and allow to cook for 4–5 minutes, until the pork is tender and almost ready. Add the ginger, fish sauce, sugar, turmeric and lime juice, and continue cooking for 5–6 minutes until the flavours infuse. Serve with sticky rice.

sticky rice

450g/1lb sticky rice

1   Steep the rice in a bowl with sufficient cold water to cover for 1 hour. This will remove the starch. Drain and rinse well.

2   Place the rice in a bamboo steamer, cover and cook over a pan of boiling water for approximately 20–25 minutes. Alternatively, the rice can be cooked in boiling water.

oriental style barbecued pork fillet
with pineapple chutney

serves 4

Pork fillet is a tender cut and in this recipe I have brought out the best of the flavour with an oriental style marinade. The sweet and sour taste of the chutney is delicious on the side.

2 x 450g/1lb pork fillet

Trim the fat from the pork. Split the fillets lengthways so that they can be opened out. Place some cling film on top of the fillets and pound with a rolling pin to flatten out.

marinade

2 tbsp dark soy sauce
2 tbsp honey
2 tbsp sweet sherry
1 dsp sesame oil
1 dsp olive oil
2 cloves garlic – chopped
1 inch root ginger – chopped

1 Mix the soy sauce, honey, sherry, sesame oil, olive oil, garlic and ginger together in a bowl.

2 Place the pork fillets in a shallow dish and pour the marinade over them. Cover the dish with cling film and leave the pork to marinate for at least 30 minutes.

3 Cut the pork into even-sized steaks, place onto the grill of a preheated barbecue and cook for approximately 12–15 minutes, depending on the heat of the coals. Turn the steaks regularly. A little marinade can be spooned over the steaks during cooking.

pineapple chutney

1 pineapple
1/2 small onion – finely chopped
juice of 1 orange
110g/4oz soft brown sugar
4 tbsp white wine vinegar
1 tsp coriander seeds
1 tbsp pickling spice – crushed

1 Peel and core the pineapple and cut into evenly sized chunks.

2 Add the pineapple, onion, orange juice, sugar, vinegar, coriander seeds and pickling spice to a large pan.

3 Bring to the boil, cover and simmer gently for 45 minutes, stirring occasionally. Serve hot or cold.

57

baked whole fish
with a 3 flavoured marinade and a cucumber and radish salad

allow approximately
110–175g/4–6oz fish per person

This marinade, which combines the sharpness of lemon, the heat of chillies and the sweetness of sugar, works a treat on a whole fish. Serve with the salad below or with the aubergine relish on page 35.

1 whole fish (900g–2.3kg/2–5lb), e.g.
sea bass, red mullet or salmon

1 Clean the fish and remove the fins and any scales. Leave the head and tail. Score the fish almost to the bone with parallel diagonal slashes on each side.

2 dsp olive oil
6 tbsp lemon juice
2 green chillies – deseeded and finely chopped
1 dsp soft brown sugar

2 Mix the oil, lemon juice, chillies and sugar. Place the fish in a shallow dish and spoon over the marinade. Cover with cling film and leave for at least 30 minutes before cooking.

3 Prepare and preheat the barbecue, brush the rack with a little oil and place the whole fish on the rack. Alternatively, the fish can be wrapped in foil before placing on the barbecue.

4 Cook for approximately 10 minutes on each side, turning only once. Cooking time will depend on the heat of the coals and the size of the fish. The fish is cooked when the flesh leaves the bone easily and can be evenly flaked.

cucumber and radish salad

1 large cucumber – peeled and diced
10–12 red radishes – topped and cut into fine strips
1 dsp finely shredded coriander or flat leaf parsley – finely shredded
1 tbsp white wine vinegar
1 tsp sesame oil
1/2 tsp caster sugar
1 tbsp soy sauce
1/4 tsp English mustard
lettuce leaves

1 Prepare the vegetables and place in a bowl with the coriander or flat leaf parsley.

2 To make the dressing, place the vinegar, oil, sugar, soy sauce, and mustard in a bowl or in a screw top jar and mix or shake well.

3 Arrange the vegetables on a dish on top of a bed of lambs lettuce or leaves of your choice.

4 Just before serving, pour the dressing over the salad.

easter day

warm salad of steamed asparagus
with buttery lemon grass sauce

serves 4

There are many different varieties of asparagus. Green asparagus, however, is the vegetable that heralds the arrival of spring. With its unique flavour it is best lightly cooked and served with a simple dipping sauce and crusty bread. If the stalks are a little woody, peel them as near as possible to the spears.

buttery lemon grass sauce

1–2 stalks lemon grass – finely chopped
2 spring onions – finely chopped
1 tsp chives – finely chopped
125ml/4floz dry white wine
4 tbsp double cream
150g/5oz butter
1dsp chilled dry white wine

350g/12oz thin green asparagus stalks
1/4 tsp salt

1　Place the lemon grass, spring onions and chives in a small saucepan with the white wine and heat gently for 2–3 minutes. Add the cream and bring to the boil. Simmer very gently and add the butter, a little at a time, and whisk well until the sauce becomes thick and creamy. If possible, serve immediately. Otherwise, remove from the heat but cover to keep warm. To stabilise the sauce and keep the consistency, add 2 dsp of chilled white wine and stir.

2　To prepare the asparagus, wash the stalks (take care, as the tips are very delicate), and snap off and discard the woody ends, so that you are left with the tender part of the stalk. If you don't own an asparagus steamer, bring a pan of salted water to the boil and carefully place the stalks into it. Cook uncovered for approximately 6 minutes, varying the cooking time depending on the length and thickness of the stalks. Be careful not to overcook or the colour will spoil. The best way to test the asparagus is to place a skewer through the thickest part of the stalk – if the skewer passes through easily, the asparagus is ready. Drain and place the asparagus on a platter.

crusty bread
rocket leaves

3　Pour the warm sauce over the asparagus and serve with crusty bread and rocket leaves.

rack of lamb
with a gremolata crust and lemon gravy

allow 1–2 cutlets per person –
rack approx 10 cutlets

Lamb is popular at any time of the year, but is traditionally served at Easter lunch. In this recipe I have combined it with some lemon, herbs, parsley, garlic and a little olive oil.

gremolata crust

4 dsp olive oil
4 cloves garlic – finely chopped
zest of 2 lemons – coarsely grated
$1/2$ tsp black pepper
2 dsp parsley or rosemary –
finely chopped
110g/4oz white breadcrumbs

Gently warm the olive oil in a pan and add the garlic, lemon zest, black pepper and parsley or rosemary. Mix lightly. Add the breadcrumbs and continue to cook until the mixture binds.

1 rack lamb (8–10 cutlets)
2 dsp olive oil

Ask your butcher to prepare a rack of lamb, ensuring that all fat is scraped away from the bone, leaving at least 2 inches of the bones bare of fat. Pat dry the flesh section of the lamb with kitchen paper and cover with the gremolata crust, patting down carefully and firmly to ensure the crust will stay on during cooking. Place in a roasting tin, sprinkle with the olive oil and cook in a preheated oven @ 200°C/gas mark 6 for 35–40 minutes. The lamb will be pink when cooked. Increase the cooking time if you prefer your lamb well done.

lemon gravy

275ml/$1/2$pt meat juices
zest of $1/2$ lemon
2 dsp honey
10g/$1/2$oz plain flour – optional
2–3 dsp water

Strain the meat juices from the roasting dish into a saucepan and add the lemon zest and honey. Heat through for 2 minutes. If you need to thicken the gravy, mix the flour with the water and stir in. Bring the gravy to the boil and continue boiling for 1 minute. Serve immediately.

roasted redcurrant sauce

This colourful sauce is quick and easy and is made with the tasty juices that have come out of the lamb during cooking.

275ml/¹/2pt lamb juices
2 dsp honey
2 dsp reducurrant jelly
4 dsp sweet sherry
2 spring onions – finely chopped
fresh redcurrants – crushed

1 Drain and strain the lamb juices from the roasting tin and place in a saucepan. Simmer until the juices have reduced to approximately 150ml/¹/4pt.

2 Add the honey, redcurrant jelly, sherry and spring onions to the pan and bring to the boil. Cook for 1 minute, then serve garnished with a few crushed redcurrants.

new world spiced roast potatoes

serves 4–6

These spicy roast potatoes are delicious. They can be roasted around the joint in the oven or cooked separately.

900g/2lb evenly sized floury potatoes – peeled
1 dsp plain flour

2 cloves garlic – grated
¹/2 tsp cumin powder
1 inch root ginger – grated
¹/2 tsp paprika
2 dsp olive oil
2 dsp balsamic vinegar
salt and freshly ground black pepper
2 dsp honey

1 Cook the potatoes in boiling, salted water for approximately 15 minutes until they are almost cooked but still firm. Remove from the heat and drain. While still warm add the flour and toss gently.

2 Mix the garlic and spices in a bowl. Add the olive oil, vinegar and honey, and season. Pour the mixture over the potatoes and give them a gentle shake.

3 Transfer the potatoes to a hot roasting dish or place around the roast and cook for 20–25 minutes @ 200°C/gas mark 6 until the potatoes become crispy, golden and aromatic. Cooking time depends on the size of the potatoes.

medley of spring vegetables

serves 4–6

This is a simple way to bring out the best of the flavour in spring vegetables.

450g/1lb baby onions
450g/1lb french or runner beans
450g/1lb baby carrots

Lightly boil or steam all the vegetables separately and then drain:

onions	5–6 minutes
beans	6–7 minutes
baby carrots	8–9 minutes

Be careful not to overcook the vegetables – they should still have a bit of bite.

lemon dressing

zest and juice of 1 lemon
2 tbsp olive oil
$1/2$ tsp English mustard

Make the dressing by placing the lemon zest and juice, olive oil and mustard in a bowl or a screw top jar. Mix or shake well. Pour the dressing over the vegetables and serve.

pea and garlic purée

A purée of fresh spring peas mixed with a hint of garlic is delicious with any roast dish.

450g/1lb fresh peas – podded
1 dsp olive oil
2 cloves garlic – finely grated
$1/4$ tsp English mustard
salt and freshly ground black pepper

1 Cook the peas in boiling salted water until tender, and drain.

2 Heat the olive oil in a pan, add the garlic, mustard, seasoning and peas. Mix well and leave to heat through for 1 minute. Place in a food processor to purée or mash gently with a fork. Serve at once.

layered chocolate cake

serves 8–10

Easter is the perfect time to treat yourself to a bit of chocolate indulgence. This simple cake is delicious and will make a wonderful finale to any Easter lunch.

approx 350g/12oz puff pastry

Roll out the pastry to a thickness of $1/2$cm. In order to ensure that the pastry rises evenly, place a circular plate (20–23cm/8–9 inches in diameter) on top of the pastry and use it to cut out two circles. Place both pastry circles on a baking sheet and transfer to the fridge for 15–30 minutes before cooking in the oven @ 200°C/gas mark 6 for 15–20 minutes until the pastry is golden. Remove and allow to cool for 10–15 minutes.

filling

175g/6oz good quality dark chocolate – broken into pieces
25g/1oz butter
2 large egg yolks
110g/4oz crème fraîche, double cream or mascarpone
1 egg white – beaten until stiff

1 Melt the chocolate in a large bowl over a pan of warm water. Be careful not to overheat the chocolate. Now, add the butter and stir until it dissolves. Add the egg yolks and mix well.

2 Allow the mixture to cool slightly, then add the crème fraîche and mix gently. Carefully fold in the egg white, a little at a time, and mix well. Be careful not to knock the air out of the mixture.

3 Chill the mixture in the fridge until it has just set. Don't leave it too long or it will become firm.

150ml/$1/4$pt whipped cream
mint leaves
chocolate eggs

4 To assemble the cake, spread the chocolate filling on one layer of pastry and place the other layer of pastry on top to create a sandwich. Decorate with whipped cream, mint leaves, chocolate caraque (curls) and chocolate eggs.

69

vanilla mousse

with spring rhubarb in its own pink syrup

serves 6

Although a little paler in colour than it is in midsummer, there is nothing to beat the flavour of the first stalks of rhubarb in spring.

vanilla mousse

3 eggs
110g/4oz caster sugar

1 Beat the eggs and sugar together in a bowl. Now place the bowl over a pan of simmering water and continue to whisk. This will cook the eggs gently and the mixture will lose the 'eggy' flavour.

zest of 1 lemon
1/2 tsp vanilla extract

2 Transfer the mixture to a clean bowl and beat well until it doubles in volume. Add the lemon zest and vanilla extract and mix thoroughly. Set to one side to cool.

175g/6oz mascarpone
2 dsp crème fraîche
150ml/1/4pt whipping cream –
stiffly beaten

3 When the mixture has cooled add the mascarpone, crème fraîche and whipped cream. Mix gently and transfer to lightly greased individual moulds. Cover with cling film and chill in the fridge for approximately 2–3 hours, until set. To serve the mousse, place the moulds in a basin of warm water for 30 seconds. Then turn them upside down onto your serving plate and the moulds should come away easily. Be gentle.

rhubarb compote

450g/1lb pink rhubarb

1 Wash the rhubarb, dry and cut into lengths 3–4cm/1 1/4–1 1/2 inches long.

50g/2oz caster sugar
150ml/1/4pt water

2 Place the sugar and water in a large shallow pan, bring to the boil and dissolve the sugar.

1/4 tsp cardamom seeds – crushed

3 Add the rhubarb stalks and cardamom seeds. Poach gently for 3–4 minutes. Do not overcook. Serve warm or cold.

desserts

individual summer berry puddings

serves 4–6

This is a very easy pudding to make. Don't be put off by the thought of lining little individual moulds – nothing could be simpler. This pudding is best made the day before. Fresh berries are preferable in this recipe, but frozen ones may also be used.

450–575g/1–1¼lb assorted summer berry fruits – raspberries, currants, cherries, strawberries
4 tbsp water
25–50g/1–2oz caster sugar
approx 12 slices white bread

1 Reserve a few of the berries to decorate at the end, then prepare the remainder. Remove any stalks and stones, and gently poach the berries in the water and sugar for 3–4 minutes until softened. Taste the mixture and add more sugar if necessary. Allow to cool.

2 Lightly grease the individual moulds or ramekin dishes. These should be approximately 6½cm/2½ inches in diameter. Remove the crusts from the bread. Cut the bread into strips and circles and line the moulds, pressing down well. Fill each mould with the cooled fruit and just a little of the liquid – not too much as the pudding will be difficult to unmould.

3 Seal each mould with a circle of bread and cover with a saucer and weight to press the puddings down. Place in the fridge to chill for at least 12 hours.

sauce

450g/1lb raspberries or strawberries
50g/2oz icing sugar – sieved

Blend or mix well the berries and the icing sugar to soften. Pass through a plastic sieve to remove any seeds.

2 dsp yoghurt
mint leaves

To serve, tap each pudding onto a plate, using the method on page 71. Pour over the sauce and decorate with swirls of yoghurt, mint leaves and the remainder of the fresh berries.

lemon and ginger bread and butter pudding

serves 6–8

This old-fashioned pudding is still as popular as ever and has the uncanny knack of reinventing itself in modern guises. This particular version has a particular zing and freshness that comes from the lemon.

1 crusty French loaf
1 dsp butter
1 dsp lemon curd
zest of 1 lemon
1 inch root ginger – finely chopped
25g/1oz sultanas (optional)
1dsp lemon juice (optional)

Grease an ovenproof dish (approximately 1.4 litres/2^{1}/2pt). Cut the bread into even slices, and spread one side with butter and then with lemon curd. Arrange the bread in the dish, butter side up, and sprinkle with the lemon zest and ginger. If using sultanas, first place them in a small bowl with the lemon juice and leave for a few minutes to absorb the liquid. Then sprinkle them over the bread.

egg custard

570ml/1pt low fat milk
25g/1oz caster sugar
few drops vanilla essence
4–5 egg yolks – lightly beaten

1   Heat the milk in a pan and add the sugar, vanilla essence and egg yolks. Whisk continually over a low heat until the mixture shows signs of thickening, then remove from heat. Do not boil as the custard will curdle.

2   Sieve the custard into a jug and pour it over the bread, leaving it to soak for 10–15 minutes until the bread softens and absorbs the mixture. Place the pudding in a preheated oven @ 200°C/gas mark 6 for 20–25 minutes until it sets and is puffed up and golden.

Demerara sugar for dusting
125ml/^{1}/4pt yoghurt or crème fraîche

Dust with Demerara sugar and serve warm with yoghurt or crème fraîche.

fresh fruit and almond tartlets

serves 6–8

These tartlets have a light almond cream filling and can be topped with the fruits of the season, such as strawberries, raspberries, gooseberries and blueberries.

225g/8oz plain flour – sieved
110g/4oz butter – chopped
25g/1oz caster sugar
1 egg yolk
1 dsp water – chilled

1 Place all the ingredients in a blender and blitz until the mixture begins to bind. Alternatively, add the butter to the flour and work with your fingers until the mixture resembles breadcrumbs. Then add the sugar, egg yolk and sufficient water to bring the mixture together. Place the dough on a floured surface and roll out to a thickness of 1cm/^{1}/$_2$ inch. Using a 3-inch cutter, cut out 6–8 rounds of pastry.

2 Line individual moulds (approximately 7^1/$_2$cm/3 inches in diameter) with the pastry. Now prick the pastry with a fork and bake blind (i.e. line each tartlet with greaseproof paper and scatter baking beans or dried beans over the base, removing the paper and beans after 8–10 minutes) in the oven @ 190°C/gas mark 5 for 10–15 minutes until cooked. Remove from the oven and leave to cool before taking the pastry case out of the mould.

filling

125ml/4floz whipped cream or yoghurt
50g/2oz mascarpone
25g/1oz ground almonds
25g/1oz flaked almonds
110g/4oz fresh fruit
25g/1oz icing sugar

1 Beat the cream to form stiff peaks. Add the mascarpone and fold in the almonds.

2 To assemble the tarts, fill each pastry case with some of the almond filling and top liberally with sliced fruit. If you wish, a little of the fruit can be puréed by mixing it with the icing sugar and passing it through a sieve. This can be spooned over the fruit tarts just before serving.

tip

If you are pressed for time, use 225g/8oz of pre-packed shortcrust pastry.

vanilla scones

makes 8–10 scones

These light, tasty scones are ideal for freezing and can be defrosted and reheated for any occasion.

350g/12oz soda bread self-raising flour
50g/2oz butter
25g/1oz caster sugar
1/2 tsp vanilla essence
175ml/6floz buttermilk

1   Sieve the flour into a bowl. Add the butter. Cut through and rub in for 1 minute. Add the sugar, vanilla essence and milk. Mix to a firm but soft dough.

2   Transfer the dough to a lightly floured surface, knead and gently roll out to a thickness of 2^1/2cm/1 inch and cut out with either a plain or a fluted cutter (approximately 2cm/5 inches in diameter).

3   Place the scones on a floured baking sheet and bake in a preheated oven @ 200°C/gas mark 6 for 12–15 minutes or until the scones are golden brown on top.

to decorate

125ml/4 floz whipped cream
freezer raspberry jam

Allow the scones to cool on a wire rack, then split in half and fill with whipped cream and freezer raspberry jam (see page 83).

freezer raspberry jam

makes 900g/2lb jam

Freezer jam has a fresh taste and a bright colour. It can be used for pie fillings, as a topping, or to accompany homemade scones. The jam should be stored in the freezer until ready for use.

1   Prepare a container for the jam. It can be stored in polystyrene or plastic containers. Wash the containers well in hot, soapy water. Rinse and dry well.

700g/1 1/2lb raspberries
900g/2lb caster sugar

2   Mash the raspberries lightly with a fork in a large bowl. Add the sugar, mix well and leave for approximately 2 hours until the sugar has dissolved.

125ml/4floz liquid pectin
2 tbsp fresh lemon juice

3   Add the liquid pectin (a setting agent available in supermarkets) and lemon juice and stir for 2 minutes.

4   Transfer to the prepared container. Leave to stand in the fridge for 48 hours until the jam gells. Seal, label and freeze. The jam should store for up to 6 months provided the fruit is in prime condition and the containers are clean.

To use, remove the jam from the freezer and allow to stand for 1 hour before serving. Jam that has been removed from the freezer should be used within one week.

83

featherlight peach gateau
with elderflower and peach filling

serves 8–10

This gateau is light and delicious and looks stunning.

1 Grease a round loose-bottomed cake tin (25cm/10 inches in diameter) and dust with a little icing sugar.

4 eggs
110g/4oz caster sugar
100g/3¹/₂oz plain flour
10g/¹/₂oz cornflour
¹/₂ tsp vanilla essence

2 Beat the eggs and sugar together in a bowl for 8–10 minutes until the mixture is light and creamy and is capable of holding its shape. Mix the flour and cornflour and then gradually sieve it into the bowl – about one third at a time – folding gently after each addition. Now add the vanilla essence and mix.

3 Transfer the mixture to the cake tin, level out and bake in a preheated oven at 190°C/gas mark 5 for 15–20 minutes or until cooked. When the sponge is cooked remove from the tin and place on a cooling tray. Halve the cake lengthways to make a sandwich.

elderflower curd

3–4 peaches – diced
2 dsp water
25g/1oz soft brown sugar
110g/4oz caster sugar
2 eggs
2 egg yolks
zest and juice of 2 lemons
1 dsp elderflower cordial
110g/4oz butter – diced

1 Poach the peaches gently in the water and brown sugar for 1–2 minutes. Remove from heat and leave to cool.

2 To make an elderflower curd, beat together the caster sugar, eggs and egg yolks in a bowl until creamy. Place in a saucepan with the lemon zest and juice (leaving 1 dsp juice for step 3), and the elderflower cordial. Cook over a gentle heat, whisking continually. When the mixture shows signs of thickening, slowly add the butter, a little at a time, whisking well between each addition, and continue cooking. Do not allow the mixture to boil – if it starts to bubble, remove from the heat and continue stirring. When all the butter has been added, take the pan off the heat and pour the mixture into a bowl. Cover with cling film, place in the fridge and leave to cool completely.

275ml/¹/₂pt whipped cream
1 dsp lemon juice
icing sugar
peach halves or small slices

3 Remove the elderflower curd from the fridge and set a little aside for decoration. Add the cream, cooled peaches and lemon juice to the remaining curd. Spread it onto the base sponge, using the second sponge to form a sandwich. Dust the top with icing sugar, and decorate with peach slices and curd.

zesty lemon and vanilla tart

serves 8

The topping for this tart can be made with peaches, nectarines or figs and, for those not counting calories, the fruit can be split, filled with mascarpone and finished off under a hot grill.

vanilla pastry

225g/8oz plain flour – sieved
110g/4oz butter – softened
75g/3oz caster sugar
few drops vanilla essence
1 egg – lightly beaten
1 dsp cold water – optional

1   Place the flour, butter, sugar, vanilla essence and egg into a blender. Whiz until the mixture comes together. If needed, add a little water to form a stiff yet easy to handle dough.

2   Transfer the mixture to a lightly floured surface and roll out. Use the dough to line a 23cm/9 inch flan dish. Leave the dough to sit for 20–30 minutes, then bake blind (i.e. line the tart with greaseproof paper and scatter baking beans or dried beans over the base, removing the paper and beans after 10 minutes) for 15 minutes @ 200°C/gas mark 6. Allow to cool for 15 minutes.

filling

2 eggs
50g/2oz caster sugar
50g/2oz plain flour – sieved
275ml/^{1}/2pt milk
zest of 2 lemons
25g/1oz butter – softened
4–6 dsp crème fraîche

1   Beat together the eggs and sugar in a bowl until stiff, then add the flour and mix lightly.

2   Gently warm the milk in a saucepan and pour in the egg mixture, mixing well. Continue to heat gently, whisking continually, then add the lemon zest and cook until the mixture begins to thicken slightly. Add the butter and beat lightly. Pour the mixture into a large bowl and leave to cool before mixing in the crème fraîche. Pour the mixture into the pastry case and chill in the fridge for approximately 1 hour.

topping

6–8 figs
4 dsp honey
zest of 1 lemon
110g/4oz mascarpone – optional

Decorate with split figs, drizzle with honey and brown under a hot grill. Sprinkle with lemon zest. If desired, a little mascarpone can be placed on top of each fig before placing below the grill.

blackcurrant fool
and crunchy almond biscuits

serves 2–4

A simple dessert that looks and tastes fantastic. The fruit can be varied depending on what is in season.

350g/12oz blackcurrants
zest and/or juice of 1 lemon

1 Purée the blackcurrants by passing them through a sieve or placing them in a blender and add the lemon juice and/or zest.

125ml/4floz whipping cream
50g/2oz caster sugar

2 To make the fool, beat the cream into soft peaks, being careful not to over beat. Fold two thirds of the purée into the cream, add the sugar and mix lightly. Taste and add more sugar if necessary.

fresh blackcurrants
sprigs of mint

3 Place a few blackcurrants in the base of the glasses, then spoon in alternate layers of the purée and the fool. Fill until the glasses are topped up. Decorate with a few blackcurrants or strawberries and a sprig of mint.

crunchy almond biscuits

makes 12 biscuits

225g/8oz butter
110g/4oz caster sugar
1 egg
275g/10oz plain flour
50g/2oz ground almonds
1/2 tsp vanilla essence
50g/2oz flaked almonds

1 Place the butter, sugar, egg, flour, ground almonds and vanilla essence in a blender. Blitz until the mixture starts to come together as a soft ball. Add the flaked almonds and pulse for just a few seconds more.

2 Turn out the dough onto a lightly floured surface and knead gently. Roll the dough out to a thickness of 1cm/1/2 inch and, using a plain or fluted cutter (2 1/2–5cm/1–2 inches approximately in diameter), cut out the biscuits.

25g/1oz icing sugar for dusting

3 Place the biscuits on a greased baking sheet and bake in the oven @ 180°C/gas mark 4 for 12–15 minutes until cooked, golden and firm. Dust with icing sugar.

gooseberry and elderflower cheesecake

serves 8–10

The combination of gooseberries and elderflowers in this cheesecake is wonderful.

biscuit base

175g/6oz digestive biscuits
75g/3oz butter
1 dsp honey

Crush the biscuits into fine crumbs, either in a food processor or by placing them in a food bag and rolling heavily with a rolling pin. Melt the butter and honey in a saucepan, add the crushed biscuits and mix well. Grease a loose-bottomed flan tin (20–23cm/8–9 inches in diameter) and line the base with greaseproof paper. Transfer the mixture to the tin, press down well, and leave to cool for 10–15 minutes.

filling

350g/12oz gooseberries
1 dsp caster sugar
2 dsp elderflower cordial

1   Place the gooseberries in a saucepan with the caster sugar and elderflower cordial. Poach gently for 1 minute until the gooseberries show signs of popping. Do not allow them to break up. Check for taste and add more sugar if you prefer it a little sweeter. Remove the pan from the heat to allow the gooseberries to cool slightly. Use half of the gooseberries to spead over the biscuit base.

175g/6oz cream or curd cheese
1 egg
juice and zest of 1 lemon
25g/1oz caster sugar

2   Beat together the cheese, egg, lemon juice and zest and caster sugar. When smooth, pour the mixture over the gooseberries and base and cook in the oven for 15–20 minutes @ 180°C/gas mark 4. Remove and leave to cool.

25g/1oz arrowroot
1 dsp cold water
whipped cream or yoghurt

3   Gently reheat the remaining half of the gooseberries in the saucepan. Mix the arrowroot with the water and add to the pan. Heat for 1 minute until the mixture thickens and the glaze becomes clear. Allow to cool and spoon over the cheesecake. As a finishing touch, serve with whipped cream or yoghurt which has been lightly flavoured with a little elderflower cordial.

thai fruit salad
in a scented syrup of lemon grass and lime
with coconut ice cream

serves 8–10

Coconut ice cream is one of my favourite homemade ice creams and it really makes this dessert. The texture and creaminess of the coconut perfectly complements the fresh fruit and tangy sauce. Just delicious!

570ml/1pt water
110g/4oz caster sugar

1 To make the fruit syrup, heat together the water and sugar in a saucepan and bring to the boil.

juice of 2 limes
zest of 1 lime
1 stalk lemon grass
1 inch root ginger – finely chopped
1 pineapple, 1 mango, 1 pawpaw,
4 star fruit, 1 kiwi fruit
225g/8oz cherries – stoned

2 Turn down the heat and add the juice and zest of the limes, the lemon grass, bruised to release the flavour, and the ginger. Simmer gently for 20 minutes to allow the flavours to infuse, then strain and pour into a large bowl. Allow to cool, then place in the fridge to chill.

3 To make the fruit salad, peel, chop and slice the fruit into assorted shapes. Add to the fruit syrup and serve.

coconut ice cream

6 egg yolks
50g/2oz caster sugar
425ml/^{3}/4pt milk
275ml/^{1}/2pt double cream
few drops vanilla essence
125ml/4floz coconut cream
4 dsp grated coconut

1 Beat the egg yolks and sugar together in a bowl until the mixture is pale and golden.

2 Bring the milk and the cream slowly to the boil in a heavy saucepan. Add the beaten egg yolks and sugar and whisk steadily, still over the heat, until the mixture thickens. Add the vanilla essence, coconut cream and grated coconut.

3 Pour the mixture into an ice cream machine and churn until smooth and creamy. Alternatively, transfer the mixture to a large shallow container and freeze until just solid (this will take 3–4 hours). Remember to stir the mixture every 15 minutes with a fork to prevent ice crystal formation.

Serve in scoops in a glass and spoon over the fruit salad and the syrup.

champagne sorbet

serves 4–6

This champagne sorbet is ideal for a special occasion. Bear in mind that alcoholic sorbets can take longer to freeze than fruit sorbets and they do not keep as well.

350g/12oz caster sugar
570ml/1pt water

1 To make the sugar syrup, bring the sugar and water to a gentle boil in a large saucepan. Stir continuously until the sugar has dissolved. Simmer for 10 minutes, then allow to cool.

275ml/½pt champagne or dry sparkling wine
juice of ½ lime

2 Mix the cooled sugar syrup, champagne and lime juice in a bowl. Pour into a shallow plastic container and place in the freezer to set for 2–3 hours.

1 egg white – whisked

3 When semi-frozen, add the egg white and mix until light and smooth. Return to the freezer to set for approximately 1–2 hours, until firm.

coloured or flavoured sugar

4 Spoon the sorbet into iced glasses which can be topped or dusted with coloured or flavoured sugar.

crimson raspberry sorbet

serves 4–6

The stunning colour of this sorbet is due to the high fruit content. Eat as soon as possible since the sorbet will begin to lose its flavour and form ice crystals if stored for too long.

350g/12oz caster sugar
570ml/1pt water
450g/1lb raspberries

1 Make sugar syrup as above. Leave to cool.

2 In a food processor, gently blend the raspberries to a purée and strain through a plastic sieve. Return the raspberries to the blender, add half of the sugar syrup, and whiz again. Pour the mixture into a bowl and add the remainder of the syrup, stirring well, before placing in the freezer for approximately 2–3 hours until it is slushy and partially set.

1 egg white – whisked
mint leaves and fresh berries

3 Remove from the freezer, add the egg white, mix well, and return to the freezer for 1 hour to set well. Scoop into a glass and garnish with mint leaves and fresh berries.

summer berries in a passion fruit sauce

approx 450g/1lb assorted
summer fruits
2 passion fruit
25g/1oz icing sugar
zest and juice of $^1/_2$ lime

Prepare the fruits and lightly mix in a bowl with the freshly squeezed seeds and juice from the passion fruit. Add the icing sugar, lime zest and juice. Toss and leave to infuse for 1 hour.

ice cream or yoghurt
25g/1oz flaked almonds – toasted

Serve in individual glasses or layer in a large glass bowl with ice cream or yoghurt and top with flaked toasted almonds.

baked bananas

1 banana
Demarara sugar
passion fruit
2 dsp black rum
flaked almonds

Place the whole banana in its skin on the barbecue. Cook until the skin has blackened and the banana has softened. Remove from the barbecue and open the banana lengthways. Place on a small piece of foil and sprinkle with a little Demerara sugar and passion fruit or with rum and a few flaked almonds. Serve with cream.

drinks

mint julep

serves 1

This drink is cool and refreshing and a perfect pick-me-up on hot days. Use as little or as much mint as you like.

4–10 sprigs mint
2 tsp caster sugar

1 Crush the mint leaves and mix with the caster sugar to produce a mint-infused sugar. Remove any coarse bits of leaves.

1 egg white – lightly beaten

2 Brush the rim of the glass with a little beaten egg white and glaze it with some of the mint sugar.

125ml/4floz soda water
3–4 ice cubes – crushed
1 measure bourbon
sprig of mint
1 cherry

3 Mix the remaining mint sugar with the soda water and pour into the glass. Add the crushed ice and bourbon. Mix again and serve at once decorated with a sprig of mint and a cherry.

thai sunrise

serves 1

A touch of the exotic that's guaranteed to bring a ray of sunshine to any day.

1 measure dry vermouth
dash orange bitters
3–4 ice cubes – crushed
1 measure fresh orange juice

1 Pour the vermouth, bitters and crushed ice into a cocktail shaker or screw top jar and shake well.

2 Pour the liquid into a tall stemmed glass and add the orange juice to taste.

wedge of pineapple
strawberries – sliced

Decorate with a wedge of pineapple and some strawberry slices.

homemade lemonade
with a dash of lime & soda

makes 1 litre

Nothing beats a glass of chilled homemade lemonade on a hot summer's day. This old-fashioned recipe still works a treat.

zest and juice of 6 lemons
150g/5oz granulated sugar
1 litre/1³/₄pt boiling water

1   Place the lemon zest and juice in a large bowl with the sugar and boiling water. Stir well, cover and leave for 24 hours.

2   Strain through a fine sieve or a piece of muslin and pour into sterilised bottles. Cork, label and store in the fridge for up to 1 week.

275ml/¹/₂pt soda water
1 lime

3   Serve diluted with soda water and a twist of lime.

midsummer fruit punch

serves 6–8

This drink has all the flavours of summer, with a hint of elderflower, whose blossoms can be found from May through to July.

125ml/4floz elderflower cordial
275ml/¹/₂pt orange juice
juice of 2 lemons
juice of 1 lime
4–6 dsp crushed ice
570ml/1pt soda or sparkling water
fruit slices, borage flowers,
strawberries and blueberries

1   Mix together the cordial, orange juice, lemon and lime juice, and leave to infuse in the fridge for 30 minutes.

2   Pour the punch into a large jug, add the ice and top with the soda or sparkling water.

Serve with fruit slices and borage flowers, strawberries and blueberries.

103

iced spiced tea punch

serves 6–8

This is a very popular and refreshing non-alcoholic drink. Good quality tea is important for this recipe.

2 tbsp tea leaves
1.1 litres/2pt boiling water

1   Make a pot of tea in the usual way. Leave to infuse for 10 minutes, then strain, leave to cool and place in the fridge.

6 cloves
1 cinnamon stick
2 cardamom pods (optional)
275ml/¹/2pt water
225g/8oz caster sugar
juice of 2 lemons
275ml/¹/2pt orange juice
crushed ice
275ml/¹/2pt soda or sparkling water
sprigs of mint or borage
apple, lemon and orange slices

2   Heat the spices, water and sugar together in a saucepan. Bring to the boil and simmer gently for 15 minutes.

3   Add the lemon juice, then strain into a jug and leave to cool.

4   Mix together the iced tea, spiced syrup and orange juice. Fill some tall, stemmed glasses one third full with ice and pour over the spiced tea punch.

5   Add some soda or sparkling water (approximately ¹/4 glass) to give this drink a little fizz. Decorate with mint or borage and fresh fruit slices.

sangria

makes 1 litre

This drink is ideal for summer. It can be served with diced and chopped summer fruits and crushed ice.

250ml/9floz water
225g/8oz sugar
1 cinnamon stick
2 oranges – sliced
1 lemon – sliced
1 bottle red wine
1 litre/1³/4 pt soda or sparkling water
assorted summer fruit – sliced and diced
ice cubes – crushed
sprigs of mint
fresh fruit pieces

1   Make the sugar syrup by placing the water, sugar and cinnamon in a saucepan. Bring to the boil and simmer for 5 minutes to ensure the sugar has dissolved.

2   Place the oranges and lemon in a large bowl and pour the syrup over while still warm. Leave to cool then place in the fridge for 2–3 hours until completely chilled.

3   Strain the syrup into a large bowl. If you wish, you can add a few pieces of orange and lemon. Add the wine, soda or sparkling water and fruit. Add the crushed ice, pour into serving jugs and decorate with sprigs of mint and fresh fruit pieces.

acknowledgements

In preparing *Jenny Bristow Cooks for the Seasons: Spring and Summer* I have managed to enlist the help and talents of many people. A big thank you to everyone for all your support and hard work. To Alan Bremner and Orla McKibbin at UTV; Bernie Morrison, producer and director of the television programme; to the crew, Sam Christie, P.J. McGirr, Billy Rowan, Mary McCleeve, Ronnie Martin, and editor Robert Hastings. Thanks also to the publishing team at Blackstaff Press, to photographer Robert McKeag and to food stylist Colette Coughlan. I am also grateful to Maureen Best, Nan Millar and Vera McCready for all their hard work behind the scenes and to Geraldine McAfee and Roisin O'Brien at Peter Mark, Ballymena.

Thanks are also due to Helen Turkington at the Fabric Library, Cookstown and Newbridge, County Kildare; to Paddy McNeill of Beeswax, Kilrea, for sourcing the free-standing dressers and cupboards; to Sally at Floral Designs, Ballymena, for the flower arrangements; to Nicholas Mosse Pottery, Kilkenny; to Christine Foy, Mullaghmeen Pottery, Enniskillen; Michelle Kershaw and Diane at Lakeland Limited; Laura Ashley, Belfast; to Hilary and Ian Robinson at Presence, Newtownards, for so much hard work in coordinating china, pottery and dishes for the programmes; to Helen Bedford at Le Creuset; Jim Patton at Red Fyre Cookers, Belfast; Millcraft Handmade Kitchens, Sydenham Road, Belfast; Sydney Stevenson Agencies, Bangor, and Meyer Prestige; and to all the family and friends who contributed to the programme and helped to make it such an enjoyable experience.

index

First published in 2003 by
The Blackstaff Press Limited,
Wildflower Way, Apollo Road,
Belfast BT12 6TA,
in association with UTV

Printed in Northern Ireland by W & G Baird Limited
A CIP catalogue record for this book
is available from the British Library

ISBN 0-86540-738-0

www.blackstaffpress.com
www.jennybristow.com